How I Became an Angry Woman

How I Became an Angry Woman

Poems by
Bianca Bargo

Accents Publishing • Lexington, Kentucky • 2015

Copyright © 2015 by Bianca Bargo
All rights reserved

Printed in the United States of America

Accents Publishing
Editor: Katerina Stoykova-Klemer
Cover Photo: Vladislav Hristov

ISBN: 978-1-936628-34-6
First Edition

Accents Publishing is an independent press for brilliant voices. For a catalog of current and upcoming titles, please visit us on the Web at

www.accents-publishing.com

To Jane Vance, for everything.

CONTENTS

First / 1
We Kissed / 2
Discovery / 3
Exorcise / 4
Ophelia / 5
He / 8
Mood / 9
Three Dreams / 10
How I Became an Angry Woman / 12
Fool Me Once / 13
Revenge Is Best Served Piping Hot / 15
I Don't Know Why I Sucked Your Dick / 16
Granny Smith Apple / 18
In My Fuck Me Shoes / 19
Mountain Mouth / 21
Bird's Plight / 22
Two Dreams / 23
First Love / 25

Acknowledgments / 27

FIRST

I felt foolish
and clumsy,
trying on sexy
like a 10-year-old
with socks
in her bra.

Losing my nerve,
I fumbled to hide
the thighs I thought
too thick to be
loved,

but he called me
beautiful,
and his blue irises
bloomed
like fireworks.

WE KISSED

till the skin
of my lips split—
tiny wounds
hair-thin and stinging
as paper cuts.

When he left
      he left me hungry;

I tongued
each slit
where the skin
had ripped,
slaking myself
with the raw salt
of reliving.

DISCOVERY

Love is a grey madness
I was never good at
suffering—
too many nightmares
of your old lover;
her fingers, dirty
with knowing you first,
stab my eyes in my sleep.
I conjure her face—
sharper, thinner
than my own—
and make for her a body
rife with my opposites.

Months ago
I found a bird
singing songs you wrote
with her name in each verse.
I shoved it down my throat
in an animal panic:
swallowed it
whole.

EXORCISE

She wants to run herself into numbness,
fight for every stabbing breath, burn
until she hears her fragmented heart
thump out warnings that it might
explode.

She wants to crunch and lift and
lunge and squeeze. She wants
the counting and routine,
to lose herself repeatedly
in three sets of fifteen.

She wants to grunt and groan and gasp,
to make those sad and angry sounds
in a place where they won't be
questioned or even
acknowledged.

She wants sweat—
a stronger salt than tears.

She wants to shed
the sullen pounds and inches
from her legs and hips and abdomen
so there will be less of her left
to love him.

OPHELIA

I.

Green was always her favorite color.
To her it was alive and thriving,
blooming and growing,
young and hopeful,
as she was once.

She wanted to go where the green was and
float beneath the surface-skimming limbs,
beside the mossy banks and the
tall, firm reeds.

She knew she herself had been too green.
She believed his love-soaked promises.
She let his fickleness and treachery
fuel her own fall into
madness.

So she donned a dress in her favorite color,
plucked a fist's flowers from the
feathery grass to take with her
to the water, and she let all
the green in her world
fade slowly
into black.

II.

In the evenings of my younger days,
I'd fill the tub a little less
than halfway

and lower myself back
into the soothing heat,
arms braced
left and right.
I'd let all my hair get wet
and fan it out gently all around
me so I could look over and see
the soft strands ripple and surge
beneath the steamy surface.

Now it makes me think of her.
I'm sure her hair looked beautiful
splayed all about her in the water,
floating out from her smooth brow
and long neck, in swirls around her
shoulders, reaching out to the banks,
clouding up the surface—
I'm sure she probably didn't notice.

III.

You should have stuck it out, Ofi.

You should've gritted your teeth
and hummed those eerie songs
to yourself.

You should have harbored all the hurt and
let it smolder beneath your breast.

You should have clenched your fists till
your fingernails left your palms bloody.

You should have hoisted up the hem of your dress
and run for a front-row seat at the final scene
so you could have seen the Danish Prince
who sent you drowning
get his in the end.

HE

has catalogued his favorite
body parts, eaten girls' hearts
like Valentine candy—
that boy's tongue
must be chalk
by now.

It *is* harder for him
to hiss he notices,
his whispers
sour in his mouth
like milk.

His fingers feel dead
as shed snake skin.
When he tippy-tips
them toward zippers
it's the sick tickle
of a spider crawl.

It makes the girls tense.
They can sense his emptiness,
but he always picks the hungriest—

he's found his niche
as a starved bitch's bone.

MOOD

> *This is a torch song,*
> *Touch me and you'll burn.*
>
> —From Margaret Atwood's
> "Helen of Troy Does Counter Dancing"

On days
like this
I smolder.

Inside
I'm all
potential,

boiling to the brim
with lava and venom.

Outside
I'm all
prevention,

barbed and twisted
like mangled wire hangers,
flinty even to friendly fingers.

Who knows the reason?
You don't need one.

You only need a
warning.

THREE DREAMS

I.

I'm flying naked through
the night-dark sky,
hovering over bodies
of water still enough
to send my reflection.
I twirl slowly to catch
my angles in the
moonlight, sing myself
Whitman-like. This is
a body to dream about—
breast   ass   hourglass—
I finger my hair and bring
it forward in silky clusters
to my chest; the ends rouse
my nipples from their
softness. I get closer
than Narcissus and
fall in.

II.

I am a backdoor woman.
I haunt the homes of taken men.
I control the prepositions:
I'm the one they are unfaithful
with, not unfaithful *to.*
They want me for my mystery,
and I'm glad to be mysterious.

I use them in circles and circles
then leave them panting as they
wipe themselves off before
their wives come home.
Sylvia whispers hot in my
ear, "That's right, girl,
keep eating them like air—
they are just as empty."
I smile
and nod
and lick my lips.

III.

I do not wake
up moist and
alone, the right
side of my bed
cold, the sheets
there smooth.
I return home
from my own
trysts, sticky
and uncaring.

HOW I BECAME AN ANGRY WOMAN

I was born honey-tongued
and eager, a soft thing
looking for legs
to coil around.

Over and over
I opened my mouth
to men in whispers,
kisses, confessions,
prayers to false gods.

I never asked to be this
pale demon with grit teeth.

I just woke up
one morning in her
scorching skin and

blinked against the burn
of new light until I understood
it was my own eyes
full of fire.

FOOL ME ONCE

shame on you.
Fool me twice
and my rage
will be
Biblical.

I will rain down on you
apocalyptic. At night,
you'll curl into yourself
like a fetus in belly juice,
but you will not sleep—
you will know I am
coming for you.

When I'm bored of
boils and bugs and
brimstone, when I think
you've suffered enough,

I will come to you,
gentle as a mother
who's sorry she must
punish her boy,
sorry he was naughty
in the first place.

I will cup your chin
and stroke your hair
with soft hands, my voice
will be lilting as I ask for

your blood-offering,
which

> before sweat shines on your top lip,
> and your tongue unsticks itself
> from the roof of your mouth,
> before you stammer out repentant
> prayers to me

I will collect quickly
as my last act of kindness.

REVENGE IS BEST SERVED PIPING HOT

in your offender's lap
as you dance in the cloud of steam
rising from his flesh, which will bubble
like melting plastic and turn the most pleasing
shades of blistered white and rose pink.

Then, with the seedy work of tit-for-tat
accomplished, it is best to dust the ugliness
from your hands, your clothes, your hair,
and walk away, the angry voice
quieted.

I DON'T KNOW WHY I SUCKED YOUR DICK

that Monday in your shitty apartment
with the window open to the warm sun
and the sound of Kroger shoppers
across the street.

It was the first time I tried to swallow
up someone I didn't love.

It may have been impulse, the sick pull
in my stomach when I stand at high windows
and feel the urge to fling myself through them.

It may have been to prove I could,
the way I would when I was just a girl—
I'd jump the creek banks pretending
I wasn't scared to wake the snakes
cooling themselves beneath the rocks.

It may have been for the same reason
I've plucked a penny from the pavement:
because it was there. And honestly
it was so delicious-thick, it reached for me
and I felt compelled to answer.

It may have been to forget myself
and the gifts I give in love and for love,
to say fuck love altogether and instead
to understand lust, own it, admit
I'm animal, driven by the gustatory.

It may have been to own *you,*
that part at least, to lap and

suck and pump it, yes,
but also to know
I could bite it off
if you crossed me.

It was probably just so I could write this poem.

GRANNY SMITH APPLE

I love this apple
for what it turns me into.

The way I look when I eat it:
animalistic—I have to curl my lips back
and attack the green skin with
incisors, bicuspids, and best of all,
the fangy canines.

I love the sounds we make:
crunch, rip, chomp chomp chomp
as my teeth scrape the core,
the gurgles and slurps as
the tart juice rushes
over my tongue
and down
my chin.

I love the way it makes me feel,
like the First Woman
who, when she tasted
this forbidden flesh,
saw what wonders lie
outside monotonous Paradise
and ran gasping to her husband,
begging him to take a bite.

IN MY FUCK ME SHOES

I think bad thoughts.
Want to use my stilettos
to pin men to walls like
knife throwers' assistants,
want to whisper,
"Don't flinch,"
then take my teeth
to their belts.

These shoes make my feet
bleed, but I need to dance in them.
They are the bliss and the sting
inseparable; the endless
gnarled frenzy of two
humping dogs.

In these shoes I am a pulsing invitation:
Fetishists, I'll let you have a lick,
tongue the toe, my treat.
Pagans, I'll take your offerings,
lay them juicy at my gorgeous feet.

I commit a long list of sins in
these shoes and
I   am   not   sorry.
Instead, I squat and smile like
a gargoyle, waiting for God
to hurl me to hell for my
bare-faced blasphemy.

And when he does I won't
have much to say; I know I'm sick,
but I *will* ask to walk the whole way
so when I go down, it will be to the sound
of those wicked sex-heels clicking.

MOUNTAIN MOUTH

When women hear my
glideless i's they thrust
their tongues through their
teeth, sneer, and think
themselves superior.

When men watch my
lips work themselves
around each vowel,
they call me *little lady*
and feel like big men
or figure me for a feisty
mountain girl that
can't be tamed.

To most,
a slow tongue signifies
a slow mind.

In the mountains, we know better.

This voice is milky thick
and moist like mountain fog.
This voice sticks to you
like pine sap.

BIRD'S PLIGHT

In the morning I'm sun-bright and restless.
The skin between my shoulder blades swells
red like baby gums as my wing bones rip through;
then I grow feathers and own the sky.

At twilight, newly restless and uneasy in the half-dark,
my belly weighs heavy with waiting eggs; I don't feel like flying
so I weave a nest to captivate a mate: in, out, over, under—
how fast my tiny heart beats, how wide my brown-black eyes.

At night when he comes to me, how willingly I shed
feathers, let my wings wither to vestigial limbs,
flesh dead-black as frostbite.

I reabsorb the nubs, become a bird bent on loving,
grounded like the penguin who mates for life,
and forget my morning flight until *he* glides
into the moonlight. Then eyes shut, beak set,
I dream all night, remembering how my wings
would slice the wind.

The next morning, I wake singing,
itchy with regrowth.

TWO DREAMS

Once, in a dream,
I rimmed your top lip
with a strip of glue,
licked it thick with
the tip of my tongue,
then sealed your mouth
like an envelope.

Without your bedroom
voice, without the laugh
I lap up like a bitch
at her bowl, you used
your eyes like two blue
thumbs; they groped
my bruised plumb
of a heart, sought to
sink themselves in
the soft spots always
there for you, secrets
I could never keep.

Last night I dreamt
we were back together
and I woke up sweating,
thick-throated and afraid
I was a shadow again.
But then I curled against
my sleeping lover when
I realized how hard my
mind whirred to make

your blur of a face, how it
could not rebuild eyes
unworthy of remembering.

FIRST LOVE

For years I chewed on it
like a chapped lip,
traced my fingers
over each memory
like words etched
in tombstones.

Today, I tested the
old dream of him
again, the way mothers
dip elbows in babies'
bathwater:

Tepid.
No burn,
not even
a shiver.

ACKNOWLEDGMENTS

"Mood," chosen as the University of Kentucky's Farquhar Poetry Award winner of 2009, was originally published in that year's issue of *Limestone*.

Special, endless love and thanks to:

Jess Cullen, my constant muse

Jane Vance, Kasia Pater, Sue Churchill, and Chuck Clenney—fellow members of the Untitled Workshop—for sharing their friendship, poetry, food, homes, and wine while sharpening these poems

Stephanie Straub, Becky Cormier, Melissa Valade, and Halley White for their encouragement and support at readings or in living rooms

The city of Lexington

My family

and

Micah, husband extraordinaire

www.ingramcontent.com/pod-product-compliance
Lightning Source LLC
Chambersburg PA
CBHW021455080526
44588CB00009B/855